Hold

Also by Scott Thurston

Poems Nov 89 – Jun 91 (Writers Forum, London, 1991)
State(s) walk(s) (Writers Forum, London, 1994)
Fragments (The Lilliput Press, Norwich, 1994)
Sleight of Foot (with Miles Champion, Helen Kidd and Harriet Tarlo)
                (Reality Street Editions, London, 1996)
Two Sequences (RWC, Sutton, 1998)
Turns (with Robert Sheppard)
                (Ship of Fools/Radiator, Liverpool, 2003)
Of Utility (Spanner, Hereford, 2005)

Scott Thurston

Hold
Poems 1994-2004

Shearsman Books
Exeter

Published in the United Kingdom in 2006 by
Shearsman Books Ltd
58 Velwell Road
Exeter EX4 4LD

ISBN-10 0-907562-83-3

ISBN-13 978-0-907562-83-2

Copyright © Scott Thurston, 2006.

The right of Scott Thurston to be identified as the author of this work has been asserted by him in accordance with the Copyrights, Designs and Patents Act of 1988. All rights reserved. No part of this publication may be reproduced, stored in a retrieval system, transmitted in any form or by any means, electronic, mechanical, photocopying, recording or otherwise, without the prior permission of the publisher.

Acknowledgements — see page 115.

The publisher gratefully acknowledges financial assistance from
Arts Council England.

CONTENTS

Touch Watch	9
Rejecting the Personal	22
Speak for Itself	27
Sleight of Foot	34
Kneading Pool	40
In the Working World	47
Cooking	53
distinctions again	54
Sounding Scheme	57
Hold	64
Rescale	70
Reading	82
Hard Bind	83
A Bowl of Fruit	84
Ars Moriendi	85
Desk	86
Walk	87
Car	88
Where is Love?	89
The Change	91
The Bridge	92
His Self-Made Triumph	93
Tonight	94
Return to Base	95
Poem	96
Statement	97
Writing	98
O Futility	99
Red Snowflake	100
Incident Room	100
An Injury Helps	101
I Heard an Accident	101
Let's Talk About Us	102
Alternate, Slowly	102
The Only Thing to Do	103
Immaturity	104

28 December	105
Poem	106
One for the Shapeless Moments	107
Adult Toy	108
Bottle	109
Easter Monday	110
The Garden	111
Examination Conditions	112
9 April 2003	113
Acknowledgements	115

This book is dedicated to Robert Sheppard,
my mentor, teacher and friend.

TOUCH WATCH

touch watch was as to is and to come
become into you touch
longing attracts spark sharp across terminal
planks lined up to splice light from
the station
where links touch towards and that
need exit to situation
not working touch your skin
perhaps working that space-fold of
chemical reaction
made up your face
attraction touch links

what releases is a chanced posture of collapse
where the mark on the floor
walks a noted glimpse
articulation demands that this be a
choice procedure where the line tails out –
don't do it for long
or it will get you

articulated transactions become unto
what you left
damaged corners on a burnt pile
sear a red stain into flooring
at once walking

walking out amongst glass flowers
slight suspension notes the increase
if you fall spiral into what is home
and known
a waking is not next to what was
formulable
decrease
out

yes say why
attach a columbine attractor
a tube down which things spread
the outer layers warmed shine
catching up on making
catching up on exercise

my sections cook a yellow
sample disc turning to well-done
this recommendation doesn't make
things easy
attempting to dive derive that route
crossing the aisles
lengthening strides

attracted anxiety
bottles up a neck-echo
of traced weakness
control is possible if you
use it for the first time
it works
you know

release an area of discovery and trepidation
a playing to rules funnels
extracts gently into a gulf of space
levels set change from one minute
to the minute
what can you try to do?
exchange support
link traces

linking slips up to boil down whole again
dramatised symptoms irk a tiring drive
what you walk is what you give
eating over to a yearning
what can I do for you
to lift walk over and
down again

full of a cage of anticipation
guessed transmission in crossed-wiring
a heated cool magnified over any
edges to fall underneath
if the two poles just missed you
why are you on this train
I can't forget your fortune
brace slides sudden
lost a coat
no pay

that contingency becomes a death-space
lithe over flurries
what we continue traced across
translation plain of attachment change
and growth
I could guess what makes
dive into
your love

where began what we could now
come to terms with
still stilled on a moving line
these two edges sped-up telescoped now
us two lying in a circular notch
rotating

ethernets bark ripping sound
in a wind of attainment
what ages approach a well of webs
moving to the top
spark a drive hole down
make parallels

REJECTING THE PERSONAL

rejecting the personal
conversations spliced out
on the return of gender
she finds a genial space
intersected locked
in the utility room
a pile of vegetables
cut with cold pickling
it's a careful role
placing wandering lines
guesses formal gestures
placed here and
wonder an approach to
the theory of fields
he guessed could
shed some illumination
how often one
arranges those elements
begs the question
gift of procedure begins

the history of metals
light glimmers under stones
gets a lock undone
and he thinks that
she should have done
that earlier erecting
a tent in which to
chisel a fossil
gap in shoulder-blades
archaeology allows one
to get one's hands dirty
echoes placing the
excavated movement

pushes and multiplies
there is a time scale
for this extraction
woods whirl the circular
enclosure gaps breathe
an open sky

studded with larks
it's not becoming anyone's
walk a motive for
arriving late not
easy with a trapped
transport pooling the
hulk made watertight
the extent of self-
knowledge a bucket
of sand marked fire
communication options suggest
shining alternatives
made of glass and plastic
splinters microscopic point
towards the installation of
mannered accents locked away
underwraps ready to be
sold into an icy
arena forget the mirror
the ending's all stuck-down

anxiety in a market hall
of encapsulations chosen
routes arrange building
on the pre-constructed
shipped overseas small

wonders of engineering
crushed into too-small
mouths the recurrent
image flickering as usual
on the back of
isolated screens expansion is
surprising but necessary
not demanded materials
exorcise the mutant's colourful
daydream of
nightmare the footsteps
retreating now how
many can be counted
time scrapes the captured
glimpses rested on knees

body language exits a
furious music drafts
in a line of exclusion
a fraught contested
floor with open admissions
sprinkled with a clutch
of dry slogans and coloured
with wind from the
vent spaces keys to
the painting wanted
a new coat cloakroom
stuck ink an array
of prints in enclosure
files propositions pronouns
a rejection of rested
speech grafted into
particulars covert logos
eased into an uneasy

interface too much
noise

paper saving a clasped
waste the landscape
negotiated her as a
pushed-out routefinder
wheel trundling roots
rounded bends in bluffs
attracted settlements
then retracing metallic
steps backward coloured
by influence the
control state monitoring
every move and well why
wouldn't it foot down
a rhythmic acceleration
pulses a generative
gift dynamic stasis
a blasted bedroom
provides resource refuge
drains cracked open
proliferate disease

colour processes out of
date same hour requires
a death dive these
inevitable distractions
it takes time to
venture out to the
cold face spitting
calm whirrings and
reassuring clicks

mould these flashing
articulations how
many names
a process repetition
organises repulsion
the reflection of this
changing works to
allow symmetry full
expression and cast
a short step measures
distance how far

inevitably another record
yet controlled again
dependent points
distil and digest a
lascivious colon consumption
projects a dense worm
of anticipation into
the architecture
kitchen maps a sequence
these tools harness
magnetized areas of
activity translating
tool into action form
ache of
glistening materials of
dark a blindfold
walk on a long pier
projection guesses forced
routes accessing options
already denied

SPEAK FOR ITSELF

speak
speak for itself
itself
no it can't speak for itself
itself
gift is a wonder
no you mask its speech
speaking for it
self speak for itself
runs past pen and through
death threatens and you say no
'zeitgeist is ordinary perception'
speaks for itself
death threatens and speaks for
yourself
the route is generating speech
patterned webs a system of obscurity
possible power walls fractured
speaking for themselves
speak for itself is speak for itself
speak speak speak speak
bone a new layer creaks songs
a wonder speaks again
for itself
buying a speech the cold
sandwiches the network doesn't
speak
for
itself
itself speak for
speak for itself
wonder of obligation death threatens
and runs past your pen runs out
threatening death and you say no

or you act speaking for I
is speaking for
you
is speaking for them
speak for itself speaks for itself again
mind weft intricacies old gestures
this clinical distance
who guesses the effort it takes
unlikely pressures influences
in the Gulf in Africa in India in Central America
in South America in Russia in Bosnia it
speaks for itself
tries trips speaking for itself
itself speaks for itself speaks for itself
this music doesn't guess a rhythm appeal
a continued masking unmasking
death threatens speech speaking for itself
speech threatens death speaking for itself
runs past pen runs mask unmasked
guess a tapped trick, well prestige
'money is what gives superheroes their power' to
speak for themselves speaking for itself
it spoke for itself
and one other
and if it's not speaking a spoken crisis
making crisis happen accessible
clueless terrorism commands public spectacle
attention disruption memory perception
this terrorism speaks for itself
this situationism speaks for itself
a transmission rhythm web it's that
simple representation speaks for itself
representation is in a crisis transmission
having spoken for itself it spoke for

itself said spoke for itself
the relations have not changed
they are merely bent said spoke
for
itself
again
and a clueless bird in a tree blown
by terrorist speech spoken who spoke
for its self speaking itself its
margins parameters hidden homonyms
drive an extra layer of sense speaking
for itself again speaking for itself
again but who is doing the excavating
and therefore speaking for themselves
knows what to expect before they find it
because that is what experts do
they speak for itself speaking for itself
and speak for themselves
a strain evident an evident strain
death threatens a strained stained bone
excavated a rough skeleton no longer
speaks for itself a gender distinction
too powerful to be expressed in a poem
equals speaking for its own self a
gender distinction unloading
well there were one or two models
around that had some use speaking for
themselves reflecting us and not them
but it was nothing we didn't already know
not speaking but speaking for ourselves
to ourselves and pronouns speak for
themselves but not for
and speaking is speaking is peaking
speaking is speaking for itself

most probably when speaking for itself
itself can't hear itself speaking
death threatens
a pen pushes paradox
do you guess get up addressee
pronoun gives a new line give up
guess do you guess or look depending
on whether you're speaking for yourself
or other is that useful
at desk death threatens pen pushes
runs out
and intervenes speaking for itself
undermining undermined undermind
a guess in an old location
interviews interview with death
death threatens speaking with
itself to itself for itself
an enquiry into rhythms and cycles
it gestures and it's unconvincing
terrorism death pen runs out
ACTS ACT UP ACTS ACTS
RUN UP OUT SPEAK ACTS
SPEAK FOR ITSELF
and the point of a surface is that
it speaks for itself
and where why does it come from
to speak a surface again a surface
speaking for itself alone on itself
by itself speaking coming from
death speaking acts act up pen
pushing death roles towards
a speakeasy skeleton history
speaking easy for itself
for the skeleton

for history
what is it you saw down there
speaking for itself again a
mouth clasps more teeth
and it's that issue tissue
representations printed covers
on newsstands somewhere near a
bomb that speaks for itself
and who is that is speaking
for itself
to itself
with itself
of itself
into itself
on itself
over itself
above itself
under itself
beneath itself
beside itself
next to itself
alongside itself
adjacent to itself
around itself
out of itself
into itself
for itself for for for itself for itself
of for itself for speech speak for itself
itself itself speak for itself probably
speak for itself speak for itself speech
speak speaking speaking for itself it's
speaking for itself speaking for itself
a guess a wonder a trapped balloon
costs a minute's glimpse a building's

prospects a sunlight's steal as ever
speaking only of for and to itself
under that spacial unit
this horizon takes a beating
curry speaking for itself
that guess cultural myth
projects a highlight contrast that
SPEAKS FOR ITSELF
and why not and if not why not
and if not well not and if not
why not why not speak for
itself
speak for itself
speaks for itself
guess death pen acts speaking
speech speaking
speaks for itself
sandwiches obligation music pen
speaks for itself
and a change in reading renting
tests and a change in reading
tastes and a change in reading
texts and this has radical new
potential for irony that makes
a gesture speaking for itself and
ought it not to
speaking for itself
running on overtime
speaking for itself
no it's not around here
speaking for itself
well it could be near that fence
speaks for itself
don't touch it or it will speak

speak for itself like moments
during improvisation it's speaking for itself
and to itself and with itself and of itself
and to you it's speaking of your self reflection
it's simplistic but it speaks for itself
I met someone once
and they spoke for themselves
spoke for itself itself actually
enjoyed speaking for themselves it
and other
speaking speaking for for for for
itself itself itself itself
well repetitions articulate a numeracy
and literacy potential terrorist bomb
speaking for itself speaks for itself
and somewhere in between there's something
it spoke to itself volume down
obviously image spoke for itself you just
listened and as normal bits hit screen
tailored dark spells of
thinking for itself speaking for itself
thinking and speaking it's speaking
for itself and I'm speaking for
someone else's something speaking
for itself it's a guess 'cos no-one's
readable anymore and everyone is
readable anymore and speaking speaking for
itself gifts of speech speaking
gift of speech
speaks for itself
speaks for itself

SLEIGHT OF FOOT

sleight of foot
               where you hung
up traces
         coax her to rest
solid glimpses
               cultivate labour to wait
as a pearl grows
                  what rocks your skin
enlarged again
                 gleaming over soil spits
quarry-canteen
               hooking over to this
venture
         one-sided figures gleam

determined branches
                    gripped in a posture of
strength attracted
                    strategy for light-catching
where breaks
                    open along that drive
pursued beyond
                    belief lingering heat
striving build
                    up again you in circles

hidden approaches
                where that folded ring
attaches anew
                hefty poles clubbed together
on that scrub
                not hidden but before
revealing attaching
                on transformations pasted up
over and down
                again colouring those areas
what you
        watch you took there
in that
        following ringing scrub-time

    strapped in
               a niche pool curved
    to flooring
               floating strikes hung found
    above opening
               halls guess-dipped in
    formal approaches
               close-ends tie up
    tight those
               extraneous exits deep up
    fallen over
               the dip wandered singing
    sting of a
               gross snatched derivatives wing

cotacked appreciation
                      strung out in that
graft of completion
                      watch a wandering pulse
sit stride over
            careful objects next to
the hatch
        who took you there
could start to
           explain but wouldn't be
necessary although
                what you smelt took
you long
      over and out again

```
attracts down
              those ages what falls
across face
              catches that turn first
trying apart
              leaving follows you across
left there
              and right again utensils
collected in
              collapsible arrays the detail
the weight
              of that corner brings
back to you
              in itself life turn
```

KNEADING POOL

kneading pool
   struck out a gift
long light for the tunnel
emptied expeditionary episode
collapsing in parochial
fleets a starr'd board slight fulling
a bow weave (explicit)
cried for openings yr
unexpected

hipp'd carved-off aspersions
track wide in a full too brim
a berth of tylkolation –
I also hold to that calling
you summ'd those lights' harness
carried it like a horse
clattering down the cobbles
speckled up dappled to fleece call
out white

worder catches basic sums
to lick harder on target;
the feeling begins –
in here i want against I look –
shot over speculations don't
require balance,
it's just that
(

I hold you; flicked back
on the slat of a tray
stunning gasps your wind as if
a breath resolved there
what to you comes
lithe in a complete box opening
the hint of a glow
the staff of a gland

waiting in safety valve expectations
radio-porter as residues of institutional
cycles what wakes to you
up open

cuts a woundstripes
an approached displacement
not culcated but indexed
simulation a possible
riotous strip into aspect
repeat pummelled retreat
panelled longing giving
into shifting a slope
maintaining

he claims it
approaches wax walking
damp into tremulous
hollows filled the
concave explicated
enumerated
a subtle leverage of
hinted speculation
you chase those numerals
hold them down around

Ictus in odyssey
    painted approach a mounting
of slack star charts and starts
wrecked that companionship to
goal into a reached ground
mowed flat

IN THE WORKING WORLD

in the working world
                      he coughs up a crusted wagon
agon in odyssey
            plaits a strong maze
of the custom built
                strong house and stable
heave it up
        grip into strong particles
the best
      and only will do

beginning a surplus
     of thick strikes in the
public pool
   watch for fighters
lengthening
   strides catching
as can catch
   can only

Rings the world
                with the vain stir
a spill of
        called-out deluge on
you spike the
            won underlings trace open
a crack line
            of deep ception baste
the spark of
            living open matter in
foundlings,
            invisible

in the age
          of sharpened distinctions
where freedom breaks
               on the regimented turns
what images a sense
           of priority the duty
over the engagement or
               escape into history begins
wandering encrypt to a
               point matchless, inescapable –
plot a ruined moment

  here healing open to
        markings but not over
  receptive speaks volumes
         booking the place the
  seat finds you
      the conceit of that
  reservation commands
        restriction, explication
  fathom the ball
      rolling down around again

instead of crafting a flower
                         a movement to lips
of dish and pool

COOKING

cooking where
           the least
transaction
       holds I leave
it holding
       where it might
be left
     personal and turning
over causes
       what lies in that
leased hold
       bright things bring
a loosed grip

⋆

⋆   ⋆

distinctions again
up until one
objects
maintaining a point
basically needing
that around
as the customary
engagement means
a walk in the park
whilst fighters melt
restored later
as ruined
surplus
out of a limb
can priority be
high on the
approach to ballast
in cultivation
the rest is down to
strikers goals
figures and grounds
the necessary
claims
approach over
subtle areas
simulating light
in discourse
on occupations
his values about things
began to articulate
confinement such as
room-sitting

considering local choice
and suppositions
beyond the centre
in a question
discordant in
paradigm and
subject
philosophy is
achieved with
reviews severing
that habit
dismantling
scribes is to
impart art
as they go to
familiar lengths
to thetic ends
enfencing the
permanent wit
figures the one
body a completely
dynamic attitude
from firm handling
and yet
detachable
from saying
our names
collected
from public
discourse
reading was
there an object
of historical
issue pockets

of writing
suggested at the end
of recent remarks
set out to chart
the high point the
rally vaguely
proves the condition
of the whole

SOUNDING SCHEME

for a top dormant
clay spike

lends statue cleared
booted

plinth vacated on
tease toe

left on aware heart
board

*

cleaned off, the folly
began my round nuances
of fear in the midst of
fast walking feud you
behind

a turn to warn and retreat
out of the glade

*

not with standing anything but a
sabretache

is the crucial

misjudged print at exact congruent
augmented third

null. or raided
shift
logic prepares coated butts

dull hits lites
I get

but not over around
or on it

*

anything but dated fantasy
on the corner
held cigarette as
darting morsel
            in swagger in the back
            of that disadvantaged
neighbourhood smoke-screen
the photo pressed cardboard bio
lending deft glances to
lithe swifts
to decay the visible

*

what is the necessary page
of produce that lends
the right air

that speaks what you always
knew and wanted to
convinces

before touch could intervene
the strategic spill of
distance

your brave purchasing ours
but lacking in the later
reading

*

stayed too long which probably how
hell finished to like your smile
and ill-advised flattering kick

shamed me to it platform dispersal
and fast perspectives reek of the
lived world far behind it

sound tiles one by one for the
formative digital increase the
hot new resolution

*

lifts numbingly in prehensile gauze
top-stripping out the séance baize
fluctuations of light and gravy flung
before the hearth

treat pencil scratchings to the big
burger fest of well-spokenness on
a dart ghost

heathen and strung out slung strumming
to take a tub-thump full on held
under kicks
of a force

to be reckoned with

*

of course on fit full stating
to curb turned curdles into riot
stations you battle where
shiny defences shield tapers
behind the lines as well as
before and afore cut tell deal
in alphanumeric clusters of steaming
wells of rice packs numbed
forefinger forfeit to the
ever-steadying increase of violence
on the pages

*

shielding for what coaxed offerings
dried in the gulch of awards
ranged to top targets

protection hardly adequate to the pursuit
with hounds rounds and pounds of pollution
you back into pack your surround sound

turf trials timed to perform in reckless
control indexed to success links cuffed
about fallen manners and left graces

shocked to stocked topped devices
full of the magical steaming goo that blasts
your flue beyond rhetorical mass delusion

*

preparing to weigh the unsolved
action on solid grounds
bound to run

on and off neat evasions rid
paste epithets suddenly
revealed

reel

*

not timed but instantly effective
the trace of furnishings stylings
mouldings of the appearance
to take advantages laden with gifts
aflow with coke spectacles and
disciples lent penance to occupy
activity as earnings

*

HID exemplary distension
contended assimilable results
trained sights seen

the letter of support
treasured in an odd combative way
for business relative to pore

sunny open band
sunk a torch beam
again

*

you and yours light slight right
to rest bereft of tenderness
in a cynical sound scheme
to recuperate is the hardest
satisfaction remunerated excavated
rescue digs on the sullen sites

to pull out the post lowering ground
a cheat to empty space of possession
through a tribute to shifty old crafts
built to last too fast to meet
cruel refusals outside the case
of hardened display affection

*

their tolerances scheme approached
me with an offer as tempting as
salient of recent compressions
and recriminations over ill
concealed consolatory compensation
for sudden
removals
look up the house excuse
directionary fumblings licking
up pole
a fan base cooling

*

not should be to wreck
tack to the north
to bring trajectories closer
via storage rings
roundabouts
& queens

HOLD

Heaved deft rain charges
to channel urges
tried in the medial arena

Meant severe fortunes smile
not enough ever
you find it too cold or too researched
      for times past

not before night fall
troubled sleep
      over receptive
plane catching
      running at night

Derived height.
Dim source lent
sabotage option
        oblique hammered reflex
culling curves

Over the top hustled exclusive
panned out territory
        facsimile survey
road safety feature
objects are closer

Your appearance stokes
the vein spectacle
pressure tied
tamped vertebrae
        let out in regard

hit on trial
        perhaps sharing the worst
oppositional traits

forgotten feasibly
speaking for us is speaking for
necessary surface appearance
        is finally and fatally everything
hung by boots

motivation by tether
        compensation ships
both sides highly learnt reinforcement
went to tried face

rose catalogue mines
subsumed as if to lead
cunning oxides vanished
at once as if at least
would hazard the reaction

scheme graft
        announced wonders
of fusion
        tales to speed
scheme freewheeling

pokes sigh
dead stock locked
barrel over falls
march to content
heart walls

out of a subtle
rather than totally or partially present
regards of care
tissue pressed
fear addressed

tough monuments prickle failed tributes
cleared theatre stalls
hot recognition
you smart
and daring smirk

tied into junction
a discarded cold
clot circulated
and decisively
revised opinion

resolving clause
planned new articles
sensed and solved in situ
was aim drawn
on subjects

or dragged units
        same saying
we go in
        don't call us
they knew

a terror ripe for repro
inductions hands down
swiped card
hindered access
to holding positions

RESCALE

1

The pit floor inevitability, maintaining the significance of the crate. I called you out over your explanation reduced by subordinating useful activity to addition of wooden, screen-printed replicas. I just found pads on spots under tracks, they suggest a comparison between heaps and the gallery display. The new size of the injury now judged under retrograde yearning. Who kept this building dormant for so long?

2

What about a raise? The ground has grown back up the hill to cover a door jamb on its shattering brink. Ticking being operational, I was talking to you about whether the oil wheel winds up. You discussed me beautifully to prevent others celebrating their friendships but by critical advocacy, quite sure of your take on the scene: reject her, attach him, move away.

3

To avoid participating in the heroic shortening of a moving body in the direction of its motion. Crates stored in a warehouse or stocked at the back of the local shop; giant pairs of trousers, light switches left. How easy it is to represent objects without significance: you will not be determined here. The distance that leaves no turn untouched, however plausible, just promoting this kind of expression was right.

4

Some about the whole thing in scale focusing dark spot quote tense against shaded spectacles. I pick at my star cuticle. Are we covered clear longing enough to reverse each annotated date saying we are not structured by estimates nor would be imitated to further engagement? Will one will out. Recall the stained shape and copy only that with the just force of even intervals.

5

Marriage is a convenience where aspiration released invites trails of utility. Repairing the freezer compartment with a double tube in a flat short hall hold. Historically we don't make cross boxes for anyone else accidentally. So it's important I'm reading you by a little house viewing in then out the window as a wave becomes a finger just before the cleaner arrives. I turn the wave at my expense. The hero gives you something: a cast of hands sing it back sing it back sing it back to me.

6

Went to project which has been shut but is funded now as low sky, as kept against profiles. The marvellous supplies subject reproduction on sudden attended heights and long drawn out tone rose in the scale brief. Any and every one is a pair – already knee lug on levered handle – the true level: hungry, visible.

7

No, don't really want to believe it either from double gang to stone blower we know a good bad joke when we hear one twin on controlling dreaming lots of narratives are reparable on one listen only. Many pieces which all seem the same my wreckage slights your wreckage stabilisers off wobble close to the sun and the closing of rows and the day is begun.

8

Enquirer identifier: I am about to touch you hear where SAID defines an agenda to put please on someone else's plate. The loud cleric distinguishes the west long ship who's trembling, for what has been sacrificed to art let it not take human shape. Constructed as if there was another world waiting in the wings clipper; a convenient weakness.

9

The board elevates the sight of cutting – not lead into flat measurement – slashed pencil case. It made me tender setting to tone of assurance lulling suspicion submitting to encouraged might. Outstandingly they swept this way, producing wonders, organising launch manners & pads: plain variety. They coincided with a field exhibition, the guest well buried.

10

I am nearly good and your noise is towed under my stable and separated minds can tell. You're more like a statue in a garden than a fairy in the field. Egg split against bread if they must be we do need to use a crack glaze for stranger recognition. Join, refer to the painter whose past heirs are accounting with you way too much.

11

If this poor flower should attempt to attach, box its mouth and send it home to check the forward thrust. If this was to affect you, how to scale ambiguity in the service of anyone, how to assimilate simplicity? When you feel big questions not when you feel small. The picture of you as if an aperture opened in the sky your face will stay the same for.

12

Waited ahead in a shop. I drank the thought of a cup. You have re-determined me. The question of how one meets calamity head on. Don't become the interpreter. Your small bound epiphany. How come you've got my level. Right dry dock. Lead body. Can & do.

13

Moon over river. Simple sounds. Am I refusing to negotiate. Fifty, a hundred years back. Even silence. How could it be worse. Register the blind spots. Beta-blockers.

14

Past my cover. Just have control. This light. Solve it with letters. Mobile is no good. Just as many words. Against that fluidity. Sights controls.

15

If the car takes you. Missing a beat. Have a few drinks. Something quite banal. A face you can't. Leaves to pavement. Features across range. Take down some details.

16

Remembering acts remembering what if it was the same person falling and showing palms of silver? The argument is no longer linear: who writes the models captions attracts silent sympathies. Dry transfer screen print.

17

The active eye provokes from what it cannot see. What if the person in the tree was me? Fear always remains. Police support group. What if the tree was a palm tree or a date palm? Paralysed force passes fuse.

18

Modality is authority: addiction to double epithet strength. What if the window was the same window? No need for solutions: against what ground can concerns emerge? THAT is its enabling tension, unjustified.

19

Mimicking flatness, children with an adult walk, laden by what GOOD bends around them. The rhyme of loss. The body and I pulled at one man rope knot bearing witness. A gap between acts.

20

We are not in pain but we both hurt. You shave in the bath I shave. How to distinguish floes across open water, leads through ice? Sometimes it takes the whole relationship just to listen to the winds all day and night. It takes all day to get from one end of the flat to the other. You charge me with looks you ask am I timeless?

21

We must work at home.

22

Finally a narrator – one who will allow you to speak in the manner to which you wish to become accustomed. I want this hero. I want him to strap on armour, to dismember face, live up to his excesses so that all I hear is how the rusting counter rusts. A constant surprise.

23

Kick boxes. These faces on the platform; what if you made an army of them, made them up for TV, put rifles in front of them? To recognise the future prefect. Patience. I don't want it open that leaves function as lungs, lifeless, ordinary.

24

The report of secular rebuff stores the record of hard-won thought. Consumed still leaves in tact visible. Not imitation but a kind of debased ideal, recollection as if objects present. What meaning is as action was taken near or far from our conscience. There gone: the range extended. A turned trick of looking awry near miss appended. The important measure not matched by attendance: start bound a tension.

25

How does one handle filth? Counter withdrawal transfers intuition into the nature of deferred expertise, communication gaps etc. Wet dream. The whole becoming a part in articulate language I hear you. Gentle breeze glancing blow. Work makes free time visible.

26

I can't bear witness: every damage is a wrong. To cut and clip the neat defender from his paper jacket linked to mountings in a scrap book will not do. Running the ground over relations buried in port work suggests a divisibility: homespun rashers light a little fire on the table. I can bear witnessing.

27

Every expression equally fine leaves still working. Stop me and trust one search volunteer worker when the personnel crash the party explanation in a diff. senset of terms. Processing versus storage power to translate, transform, take on water. Distance allows forces resonance on all sides, what have you turned your hand in.

28

The longest possible take possible vision
Take tenses between rush to verbal take
Between rush to plastic take on whole
Reception hold against production hold
Impose will to tame holding near role

Or far from the hold made for each
Other made for another one to hold.

29

Some thing that really addressed me. A limited run of shifts re-determined and a lost line emphasising the difficulties over sure ties. A wariness as a vital organ as far as the eye can see is what people desire not smuggled in a tram car for truth. Not object giving info – is the chair actually touching the ladder? There is no project, so how to conquer? One-sided figures screen situations without too much minor necessity.

30

After turning on our moment of error we'll collect it. I'm not going to argue with you over how much is conventional how much. Absolute fear of the scale that establishes real measures. If you want to speak to me effectively never speak to me directly. The overthought at night urge to retire, pride swallowed, parade through the ventilation, the secrets turn out to be nothing. The crowd tests offering what he invites but withholds, enabling tension? Leave it out.

READING

for Ira Lightman

THE WORLD BEFORE them was of one speech and one language. The people were one and nothing was restrained from them which they imagined to do. Confounded. Whereupon poetry must try to bridge differing accounts of reference in language, that which is predicated on an object to that which is predicated on the world. Whereupon marriage must try to bridge differing accounts of communication, that which is predicated on self as object to that which is predicated on self as process. The marriage learns to teach society around it within it as together upon a peak one's lives are all before one twin. I'm not sure I can accept the painted paradise, the deferral of that uncrossable ocean to unreachable haven: it seems to sell the short attempt as if to say yes we had already arrived, we had all the time securely. Timeless sense whatever the institution. Yet we are institutional in augurations. Time essence. That your metaphor bonds the species speaks volumes of space: deferral from referral. Not interrogate but have the shape with which to look compare to a summer's day against which you are both less and more lovely. Run a line depth sounding the ocean where each kind doth double its own resemblance find. I'm not sure how you cleave marriage form family form relationship if we are to be as many people to one another as we can. Want to enjoy. I want a hero. There's a universal metaphor for

HARD BIND

Collecting the new bound text
of uncertain shape; the possibilities

have multiplied beyond management.
At this point I am paused between

having to adopt a client's taste
and having a professional's eye.

But what is that eye and body
attached; stiffened into mimicry

of the material imperfections of objects?
Is this anything I can use

against the blank sheets the boards enclose?

A BOWL OF FRUIT

Und wars für diese schon zu viel, das Aufgehn?
   – Rilke 'Die Rosenschale'

What comes of making something so
unnatural?

From the violence of an unpassed course –
a bowl of fruit.

Held heavy in blunt planes
a bunch of clustered objects in the mind.

A steady inwardness draws them in
pushes their clumsy order out

into the cosmos.

This junk
too far from space
is space itself.

Held together
it disintegrates.

ARS MORIENDI

It is too late to research;
I just don't have time.

You will have to do that for me,
Afterwards. To check and see

Where I lie up with these tracts.
Historicize me. It seems that to

Confront my worst fear – of facing
A self-inflicted death – is what might

Lead to real living with others.
I am not dying yet we are all lying

Still.

DESK

At my desk at night,
looking up at my reflection

in the skylight; I look out
of place, too young to be there.

My immaturity co-exists with
my maturity – faced by this

your adulthood collapses
into childishness.

You try to hold me to it
for fear of having to grow.

You despise your song
because it is not yours.

WALK

Leaving the house for a walk,
coming down the steps I dart

in front of someone passing.
Up below the cathedral –

the estuary looks landlocked.
On my return, before

the crossing, someone runs
in front of a car.

Making my way across,
I feel resentment.

CAR

A car overtakes,
someone shouting 'Get over!'

as they pass on the inside. I
show my finger. The car slows,

a waving fist. We slow,
it carries on. I'm sorry

I risked a beating but
who's on the right?

WHERE IS LOVE?

I

Where is love?
          Love has lost its way.
While in my heart its blind trueness
Sharpens like a needle every day.

If love is that name we give to
The best part of ourselves;
It's there when I choose to share
My dust with insects, their lives spare.

But not spare. Why should I be able
To choose? The quivering needle of an
Old compass points in the opposite direction –
It's been buried for too long.

Love has to be absolutely fought for:
To be cut out, lifted, poised
Aloft for a float in clear sky
         – it is the last word.

II

Where is thought?
          Thought has shot its last bold bolt
Twice in a heart-tree, its bland tiredness
Pulses like a minor motor way.

A blunt tab is that we pull over
Put upon the ruined counter
The worktop of choice with a charred
Coaster, a cracked lip, a screwdriver.

Buy not share my shoddy ware able to
Booze quivering guts in a holo-deck.
Starry points direct wrenched bridges
Burdened of hid samples.

Thought has to be absolutely feared absolutely
Cutting out on a free way chip board.
Trapped lights pull a float under
     – it's peeled off today.

III

It's lost that thought.
     It's shorn shod bold into a dry well,
Told twice to heat ray treatment for blind
Pulses in a ratchet mirror glance.

A heaving tub is what lights us
Pulled off a stripped sideboard.
The anvil of solace: a manky
Toaster, a bulging drawer, a flaming

My not share in dull life housing to
Snooze cruise a stunning blonde with
Several points northern direct trading co.
Busted triumphant.

That has to be it now tried to
Cut it out on the hold lamb supper
Of trawled bits negotiate the dive
     – the large day.

THE CHANGE

Why does it need to be stated?
As if it were ever any less

than obvious. That time is past
now. It is still

here. Calls and conversation echo
in the street. I no longer want

to abstract these things that
impose their attention on me;

that I impose my attention on.
That was a way of avoiding

responsibility for them, for me, but also
a way of changing them.

The change still has to take place
at a different price. A diction cut

for a clean address: the swish discourse
nails a voice. But wobbles, cleanly

on it, off of it.

THE BRIDGE

Book by cover lover lodged
lugged drawn into fallacies –

is yours a true one? Deep
rich or a shadowy shower

sunk wrapped wafer-thin around
a barking empty cask?

You stifle me the air full of men's
voices I can't wade through can't

even meet the mettle of
persuasion to cycle out lithe

platitudes cross lumps of ornate
fretwork a tight rope bridge

of tight hope.

HIS SELF-MADE TRIUMPH

does not want to articulate itself
easily does not want to close
certain doors shifts
uneasily between preparing
a welcoming house
to calling a sibling
to pitching the offer to that
caller and this one

tries to reconnoitre itself
sullenly soundly around the
lip of water's edge; totally
innocent, circumscribed
tensed up, a bit shaken
wants to lend itself again

TONIGHT

It was here where I held it –
a stubborn prick came across
plain: an hourglass ecstasy. It
bent itself for a hair pin gland
your looks heaped under stripes

Too full this attention for what
was actually straight negotiation –
taking a cab right away for a change
spanning a mere evening

RETURN TO BASE

An even silence shifts
to accommodate me. I
take it out this space
hire it as a dog
cart across the fields.
Away through birches.

Too simple trains of an
arrested motion –
under the concrete
underpass. Stuck waiting
shifting slowly the weight
the heel the knee

the hip

POEM

lay hold of an unlikely
word to face the blunt
emotion

die cast: the hot metal
springs out at last
visible

this rough hewn shape
between us sits a
gleaming form of

utility

STATEMENT

It is a matter to absorb seep in
a rough loud excess only gotten by
itself versus the cold hard reasoned line

skim of a jar's maw
opens body's pore to more

leads into a time against reflection
where clarity is only always action

WRITING

that versus the cardboard cuts
out of memory pinned to backing

your image where our day lit
with back to back annotations

sets us a part apiece; not con-
joined but rotating concentric notches

where a look flares abdomen's shriek
of claustrophobic flight or boredom's

cruising damnation. Trod lightly bound
by demeanour a meeting only under

taken for a wager of tough trust
and heartless gulps of stop

tension torched to bemuse, amuse

O FUTILITY

this silence wants to echo
formatively into another not
beset by acts of rich attention
the gold-plated nib

but fully-armed in realms of
action, the tension dissolved in a
clarity of utility

the not-yet summoned several senses
want to quit, the hired stakes
beckon to a fluid response

and yet face up to scratch
reality's surface: the non-committal
conspiring rights to that which
someone else seeks to defend

RED SNOWFLAKE

Caressing the shapeless instant glides into duration. The disaster was just a plume of smoke from here: I didn't know what language I'd been hurt in. Resistance to a mental shot let the other speak an eye taut beneath the headband of various accurate practices. Emotions in poetry are no different to those in real life – a register of shifting relations of permanent significance. Those serious convictions, however, may turn out to be no convictions at all.

INCIDENT ROOM

Visible history a fireproof depository where the only story is loss and the work as broad as the flat of the land. All the light coloured through a stained window. Adjust your technique according to the conditions. Use the people around you. Leave yourself a bit of room. Left to get leaflet from a separate sheet destroyed: one line scrolled along the edge of a bible promised to demonstrate the house style. Disremembering the childish adult, that constant disaster between dish and home, between wish and room. The church said show me the wound on the forehead.

AN INJURY HELPS

Ideal form yesterday, the only challenge is to build the scaffold – locked into scale. What categories have you got? Are you registered, pulled by the ups and downs in first class? Demand to be recognised: make a double sacrifice of pleasing pain, allow natural variations to work within yourself. Have I overstepped my bounds to endorse this designer's intentions? Yes, this couldn't be one real voice only. Has the line ended?

I HEARD AN ACCIDENT

Thinking of love in some way the other might, I thought sleep. The higher the lower the middle the landfill overflow. At least you still know what moves you. Winter is spring bound – a resolving decadence. Or am I missing local variation? Compelled to call to account: fantasise some future break. Person degraded by form, one realistic. Please lick refresh to hold down noise against the fear. Are you near?

LET'S TALK ABOUT US

A recoding of a bell ringing – a clap of fanatical attitude. A fielder runs down the side of a mountain in possession of mouth, nose. Quick flash guard day; a magpie hiding bread under leaves. My personality is home before me, a healthy limb amputation. Recognition is critical: memory is of another person. Now is good: dreams based in a real future. Your determined song abounds by me – rapid grab, quick cure. Not plenty but knowing enough about you.

ALTERNATE, SLOWLY

Looking back, in the way of being guided. A normal single fingered custom constant memory. Tough thing is lack of a strong draw right now – informed emotion recovery. Ten pages together even though you age at normal rate. Soundless altered damage heelguard standstill. This late light in late September. Rose, balanced on the banister. You are a total fluke. Collect but not accumulate – not secured by consensus nor sealed by death.

THE ONLY THING TO DO

Wreck a subject because it serves
to grimly insert oneself into history –
literally a feeling of shapes,
smooth blocks of colour: the memory
of a feeling or its reoccurrence.

I cling to my weakest
knee, a gentle buckle –
my daybook practising description
without me.

How difficult it is to generate
an account of desire,
when the erasure remains
part of the measure.

IMMATURITY

The alternative deadly superiority throws off
An offer exchanging the reward for another
Less desirable. I am forced by myself to feel
In your face a unit suffering of attended
Audition, a trap I have grown into. The performance
I left without a word hardly bolsters a living
Income. It has grown inside me and choked out
The invitation unrenewed nothing explained.

They baste they squander charmingly the wound
I can still feel as a fierce bite, a black conviction
Crushed and taut against the vertebrae. A morning's
Quick pace dedicated to a cause not my own keeps

My legs awake. I don't want to feel superior to
My friend who respected me who emigrated
Needlessly. Where have I learnt this harsh
Bitterness from? How can I escape the superior
Part of myself?

28 DECEMBER

The problem with the vessel is that a single drop always escapes – sliding down the outside after pouring. Earlier on I felt trapped by the realisation that my constant self-judging is only that: it has no transcendental significance or value, it is not a monolithic object that I cannot pass; it is just something I bring on myself, a habit I've got in to. I am writing this in order to try to deliver myself of myself: to escape the trap of my limitations by offering them to others to supersede. The poured-out volume always leaves a trace; sliding quietly off somewhere, staining the tray it rests on.

POEM

The feeling of a constant cut out
comparison – the fragment of another I hold
in my head beats me dead hands down.

What defence is there against this? Two
routes – I am worse or I am better and I am
between the two of you.

The top rots – the care I took on every book
just so much wasted time compared to the
trained, agile gutter.

Habit takes a long time to break; softly, a
pine wheezes, scrapes, a few grains tumble
off the top of the heavy dune.

ONE FOR THE SHAPELESS MOMENTS

My heart is so full in this condition
In this condition that I write in
A full heart in condition take on
For condition a past welts right
In the throat it wishes to join
What in a rate heart wrote
It sounded wrung out tampered
With not quite right a white
Wash out

                But a ring dances for
Me pulls me into its protective
Causes a catch pin numbering
Its sufficient causes caught me
Unawares in the reconditioned
chamber

ADULT TOY

If that anger is colloquial ought it not to be transcribed?
Off the gleaming edge of a rim shot I'm making strategies
which are more self-protective, flexible bounds stiffly into
silent shape – MY WINGS THE LIP OF AN HORIZON

Tears into a cup a faithful construction keeps me quiet.
I am a gate which is not open. I am on the threshold of
A novitiate for a profession in which there are no
Novices. The only game in town page of cups unhooks

Me. If I don't take responsibility for my feelings.
If I don't share responsibility. If I make a toy of thought.
If I see the expression of anger as a fantasy out of fear.
If the statement catches what is necessary it becomes the

engine for movement. Your seriousness generates a
reactive levity in me – I would smile or laugh to combat its
hideousness. Flick the fucking switch.

BOTTLE

In the mouth of my new water
bottle there is a flaw – a trick of
flicked flashing on the screw, a little
fin that catches a light's breadth.

It provokes me. The flashing cuts into
the softer tread of the plastic stopper:
scoring lines. I fear this marred
perfection. I determine to return it, but

break a patterned habit against the
stress. If I can accept this flaw
I buy in myself a bigger store: a
stock of held resistance.

EASTER MONDAY

Outside the church, a mass through the mushroom of a speaker. A tense perimeter tried by perambulator and mildly embarrassed adolescents. The organist's voice comes over a toneless cackle. It ladens it down, this ventriloquy of the absolute: boils in my brain until I calm myself by staring at the regular blocks of paving, intact limitation. What blossoms out above my head is the most or perhaps the best I could hope for. Bright sunlight on the petals against a blue ground suspends time: registered only by a shadow falling.

THE GARDEN

If the epiphany stuns it can
hardly be felt. Let it be out
here. Walking up to the white
plaster walls of the gate; all

that remains of the demolished
lido, apart from a few shattered
chunks of brightly painted concrete.
This ruined world is free to be

reinhabited, but by whom?
There to walk without a mate?
It is not without people in a sense
but saturated with an ego trying to

isolate itself from a former ideal.

EXAMINATION CONDITIONS

Again a room: this time a head still
vision expands to guarantee a depth
which places the human on a pedestal.

But what a pedestal. The sports hall
shabby and ill-lit: the performances
of grand athleticism framed by

broken chipboard and loose wiring.
The overlapping lines of different games
all join in a pattern thanking god

for the degrading of the human.

9 APRIL 2003

This statue is hot.
Expansion joints creak open
in desert sun. Emotions come
over a shelf of sure blocks
and second starts. A hasty noose
is made available.

Face covered – the eye thrust up winks once
and proudly weeps, the emotions have gathered
on the surface; softening its blow into
history. They are softly dropping
dew; they are fully present in
the heart

Face uncovered – cups a poised vial
of recollection, a flexible pose: feeling
the same old conducting loops. This is
evenness; respite despite
the blasting wind
of the sand storm

Nothing remains beside this
murderous creation. A torn
away wishbone spills its viscera,
a sole slapping its forehead.

Ackowledgements:

Some of these poems have previously appeared in the following magazines: *And*, *Cul-de-qui*, *First Offense*, *Freebase Accordion*, *Garuda*, *Great Works*, *Maquette*, *Pages*, *Poethia On-Line*, *Poetry Salzburg Review*, *RWC*, *Spanner*, *Staple*, *The Gig*, *The People's Poet*. Thanks are due to their editors.

'Sleight of Foot' and 'Kneading Pool' first appeared in the 4-pack collection *Sleight of Foot* (Reality Street Editions, 1996). Thanks to Ken Edwards and Wendy Mulford.

'In the Working World' first appeared in *Two Sequences (RWC* 42, 1998). Thanks to Lawrence Upton.

'Where is Love?' first appeared in the anthology *Listening to the Birth of Crystals* (Paula Brown Publishing, 2003). Thanks to Alan Corkish, Andrew Taylor and Paula Brown. It was republished accompanied by untitled appearances of 'The Change' and 'The Bridge' alongside 'Hard Bind', 'A Bowl of Fruit' and 'Ars Moriendi' in the anthology *The Allotment: New Lyric Poets* (Stride, 2006). Thanks to Andy Brown and Rupert Loydell.

'The Only Thing to Do' first appeared in the anthology *Onsets* (The Gig, 2004). Thanks to Nate Dorward.

The poems on pages 93-102 first appeared as *Of Utility (Spanner* 42, 2005). Thanks to Allen Fisher.

Thanks are due to Peter Manson for producing the hypertext version of 'Rescale' at *Freebase Accordion*, viewable at www.petermanson.com

Thanks are due to Miłosz Łuczyński for his slides of computer-generated visual treatments of my poems which accompanied performances of 'Speak for Itself', 'Sleight of Foot', 'Kneading Pool', 'In the Working World', 'Cooking' and other poems at the Śródmiejski Ośrodek Kultury in Kraków, Poland in May 1997 and at Sub-Voicive Poetry in London in January 1998. Thanks to the organisers Elżbieta Wójcik-Leese and Peter Leese of the Jagiellonian University in Kraków, and Lawrence Upton in London.

www.ingramcontent.com/pod-product-compliance
Lightning Source LLC
Chambersburg PA
CBHW032055150426
43194CB00006B/540